EMAIL EPISTLES
PoetKen Jones

I0172906

ISBN-13: 978-1-948712-44

© 2019 Ken Jones

Cover photo by Raxon Rex/Flickr via CC
Composite image based on photo of "Horse and Rider" by Patrick Gries,
taken in the Muséum national d'histoire naturelle,
blended with fire textures by suicidecrew and Fire-Love-Account,
both at www.deviantart.com.
Image has been flipped horizontally.

Layout and Design by Susie Tommaney

Weasel Press
Manvel, TX
www.weaselpress.com

Printed in the U.S.A.

INTRODUCTION

Prompts are common features Creative Writing teachers use to offer inspiration or form to students, a jump start to the poetic process. As a Professor, I used them frequently, but in my own work-almost never. Until a couple years ago when I began a series of responses to what was appearing in my email inbox from poetry pen pals near and far, some of whom I've never met in person. After a recent health scare, I realized how much I valued these verse exchanges-and how much these almost daily diversions had become a major part of my creative output. Hence the book you hold in your hands.

Thanks to all listed below whose own communications inspired these pieces-first and foremost "Spirit" Thom "The World Poet" Woodruff, who started me on this path with his astonishing fecundity. Also my gratitude goes to Angel Abitua, Michael FitzGerald Clarke, Kat Copeland, William T Dawson, Jonny Greene, G. Fowler, Desiree Henley, David Knape, Alex Krysinski, Neil Meili, Anne Seite, Ed Seymour, Connie Williams, and the team behind Transcendent Zero Press-Dustin Pickering and Z.M. Wise.

I also have deep and abiding respect and gratitude to Weasel Patterson for publishing this book-my 2nd collection on his Weasel Press, as well as to the beautiful and talented Susie Tommaney, who has worked on graphic design and cover art for numerous projects of mine over the years.

While refining this manuscript for publication, I realized these poems offer insight into my daily physical and intellectual concerns as well as a snapshot of the chaotic times we all share. I hope you enjoy this freshest bread from my poetic oven-hopefully they will offer you a bit of sincere sustenance as well.

PoetKen Jones
June 2019
Gonzales, Texas

HEBREWS 3:13

Encourage one another daily, as long as it is called Today,
so that none of you may be hardened by sin's deceitfulness.

TABLE OF CONTENTS

RE: "THE PLACE OF CANNOT"
THE PLACE OF CAN

"The Gates of Hell is my favorite Rodin sculpture" —
PoetKen

Evil is reality in stone
Stone made evil reality-and space
Is an extraordinary hell- outward rocks
Visible in quarries of multiverses
A disappointed God (as One must be)

Bathes in astonishments constantly in darkness
No face, an unknowable Tao, mere darkness,
Eat the never finished stopped moment
A filthy Earth with a graffitied exit
Free will in myriad excuses.

The pearl of our moon, our souls vomit
Under hells or a dozen simulacrums after
Water and magma freeze lost-our erased misnomers
A tombstone etched with a definite lie-
Pain has no name and has assistance

When our moon goes our bindle stick will appear
But the smooth infallibility we know we
Think is the transient fermented dregs
Of found. I flow from gnosis understanding everything
Clothed on the mountaintop.

RE: AFTER 8 DAYS IN SETON HOSPITAL

Thinking you're dying in the hospital
Common time's near fatal lull
Stinking, lying in bloody fecal material
Senses newly awake yet dull
You hear every artificial beep beep beep
Of live giving machines stopping your sleep.
The nurses come to check your vitals
The kitchen arrives to fetch your vittles
Your hear your next door neighbors retch
Wonder if they're closer to death
Driving you to frantically search
For a pen to write your final verse
Before they call for the next hearse.
Today a six week old kitten attacked
My thigh, broke the skin, I pushed him back
Then watched the blood flow red
Laughed then kissed him–I wasn't dead.

RE: NO STRAIGHT LINES IN NATURE

As I lay in pain with every motion
My broken life unable to reset
I wonder–did the wild birds of emotion
Fly me into this hurricane of regrets?

RE: IT IS NOT AS IF WE CAN DO AS WE PLEASE

Even Elvis had limits.
He could fly peanut butter and banana sandwiches
On his private plane from Vegas to Memphis
But needed Dr Nick to shit them out.
My favorite part of Graceland
Was the guest house in the back
With the hundreds of gold records
From all over the world on his wall
What profiteth a man to gain the world
But lose his own soul.
His planet shaking music
Synthesized black and white sounds
That surrounded him like air in his youth
Leading a social revolution of race, class, gender
While he died on a toilet in a pharmaceutical bender.
After "That's All Right, Mama"
Hit the airwaves the story goes
Elvis was at the movies
His mama had to tell him
The man at the radio station called for an interview
Because his phones were blowing up
The DJ made sure to stress
Elvis went to Humes High– the white school
In highly segregated Memphis.
Elvis said he just did what came naturally
Sam Phillips said If he could find a white kid
With the black sound he could make a million dollars
But he sold Elvis' contract for $35,000.
While Elvis made millions yet died in misery
And former carnival barker Colonel Parker
Took half....

RE: SOURCE

This shallow and frail town
Where I was born with a crown
But now live in as a clown
In God's ferocious waters drowns
The dreams of all who stay around.
Now hear with ears the sound
Of mother's fists pound
Hospital tables as baby drops down
To begin again life above ground
Only God knows if he will rebound
Know that loss and pain will surround
No matter what happiness is found...

RE: A PRETTY PICTURE

A man told me once when I was rude
"Life's all about your attitude"
Since that day I've leaned toward the light
Found the happiness in the daily fight
If ever saw that man again
I'd shake his hand and be his friend..

RE: FWD: WILDE,BEWARE!Y

We are headlong into the Sixth Extinction
Most humans blindly ignorant
That Homo sapiens isn't immune.
My girlfriend has been watching Zoo shows
On Animal Planet– they move around New York
From Queens to the Bronx to Central Park
Healing penguin chicks then releasing them
Into their climate controlled cold water habitation
A simulacrum of their natural environment
Except for being bullied by their elders
Pushed off the rocks into the fake lake
Like kids being tossed off the high dive
At the local pool this summer.
As the temperature rises inexorably
Will those children have their own offspring
Or will they be the final generation
To know a Wild planet, a living Gaia,
A breathing vibrant life besotted sphere
Soon fever dead for our convenience?

RE: ERIK KENNEDY ON LES MURRAY – BERFROIS

I don't know the man or his work
But "Subhuman Redneck Blues"
Strikes me as a great title. And I agree
That politics make poor poetry
And to trust the art not the artist
But is our polarized times
An anomaly or an analogy?
Regardless, I think Murray was right
That if we're lucky any poet
May get a dozen poems that survive.
I heard recently that Donald Hall once said
"I was 38 when I realized nothing I write would matter
Or survive me" and he kept at it for 50 more years.
So we write for ourselves, and others we share it with,
And live each day as best we can.
Today I read in Conroe for Walt Whitman's birthday
A man who most people didn't know when he was alive
And is now considered America's National poet.
So I will read for today's audience, write for myself,
And pray for another tomorrow...

RE: THE CHRONOLOGY IS CONFUSED

The chronology is confused
My Mom complained when I asked her how she was today.
At ninety she has none of the elder infirmities expected
But she still can't muster an "I'm fine". So I rejected
Her absurd pity party because I almost passed away
Recently at an age not considered young but not old either
And I've certainly never been accused of being a Pollyanna
But if that term whizzes at me like a pitcher's tricky curve
I won't duck backwards or deny it neither
As I now see every day as Earth's own delicious manna
And heaven, hell, or death are easy to survey if you have
the nerve...

RE: THE MECHANICAL CIRCUS OF SOUND&METAL&LIGHT

As a small town Texan child
The traveling carnival offered escape.
I would go just because our bleak landscape
Suddenly blazed bright and wild.
I could win prizes at the ball thrown horse races
Watch the scared yet excited faces
Of other kids much bolder than I
Who would find their favorites then ride and ride
While I threw up on The Zipper and started to cry.
Once a trailer of aborted fetuses In alcohol jars
Stood like a local metaphor among the abandoned cars.
The barkers said their mom's had done too many drugs
Suddenly, all I wanted was my mother's hugs.
Instead I went home, sat at the piano in the living room,
A lonely spot I knew as my future dreams tomb
And wrote a song called "The Sideshow"
Wishing I had some place of freedom to go....

RE: ADD YOUR NAME: WE MUST ADDRESS FACEBOOK'S DANGEROUS CONCENTRATION OF CORPORATE POWER

I hate Facebook
The way it steals your data for corporate profit
And the machinations of the surveillance state
I hate the way it dredges moments you were glad to end
I hate the ease of LIKE and SHARE where people pretend
They'll appear at your gigs but never do.
I post nothing on social media and you
Might call me anti-social
But I prefer the actual "meat space" interaction so
Much more than a cyber cell hell
Where you really can't tell
What is true or faux or yes or no
Except when told by some billionaire Millennial
Financed by the CIA and hiding algorithms meant
To crush real dissent
Behind a wall of false pious PC proclamation
That aren't even an approximation
Of lived reality as now even Generation Z
Can see, comment on and mock- only to be banned
In what once was a proudly free land.
And anyone who relies on Facebook
For accurate information or an unbiased look
Into what's happening on our ship of fools
Deserves this manipulated high tech tool...

RE: THE BOY IN HIM

When my girlfriends said
"Will you ever grow up?"
They were hoping the kid was dead
And the man would show up.

But I answered back
"Adulthood's not always for me
As the maturity I lack
Makes for fun and creativity"

Sometimes I can be a man
But it's still in the plan
A part of me remains Peter Pan

RE: WELL(I DO NOT AGREE!)

I can't agree there's always a choice
Sometimes people are robbed of their voice
Not in a Calvinist predestination
More like stuck in a run down train station
One line runs toward a vigorous past
The other a future that won't really last
We sit with our ticket already punched
Breakfast a memory, eating our lunch
Dinner coming faster than we wish
Until we reach our Midnight Snack dish
We say a short prayer over our Last Supper
Thankful for a life of joy and succor
We hear the final departure announcement
Disappear through a door; no one knows where we went
The left behind stare at their own boarding pass
Waiting for the call and their own last dash...

RE: SPRING RAIN

Booming thunder drums
Bring Frightening lightning
Raindrops sing of Spring
Then dry calm comes
Today is yesterday's tomorrow
Time to wipe away the sorrow
Greet the Sunshine with open arms
Count your blessings and lucky charms..

RE: "CLASSIC" COKE

Have no fear
The thought police are here
To replace the so called classics
With their latest language trick
Consigning dead while males
To the dustbin of history's scabs
Like Moby Dick-great white whales
Killed by P.C. Ahabs

RE: "WOKE"

The Vatican has walls
To protect the stolen wealth
The Catholic Church robbed
By force and stealth
Yet the pope has the nerve
To lecture the masses
Maybe he should trade his hood
For some self reflecting glasses...

>⋯⌣⌣⋯<

RE: "FIRST THOUGHT=BEST THOUGHT!"

The Catholic Church
Sits on a perch
Of stolen gold and treasure
Behind tall walls
They lecture all
On guilt and wealth and pleasure
Yet when it's pointed out
They dodge and shout
Spin, obfuscate and weasel
But remember Jesus what said
For the rich and well fed
About heaven and the eye of a needle...

RE: MOON OLDER THAN BURNED CATHEDRALS

Cathedrals burn
Mother Earth turns
Full moon Friday night
Sister Luna lends her light
Those who once were alive
Haunt the shadows of our hive
We still trapped in this realm
Cry tiny and overwhelmed
Today we bless this existence
Wait for evening's satellite dance...

>✗✗✗<

RE: LANGUAGE AS ASSAULT

They live in the Gaslight District.
"You're crazy! You're sick!
You're just jealous and insecure.
You're too sensitive, for sure.
I was just joking.
Why are you choking
On my funny words?
Pretend you never heard.
Let it go.
It's time to grow.
Lose your phony fear.
You're the problem here.
I never said what you think.
It's your fault you're on the brink.
You can dismiss this email as spam
But I know who I am".

RE: NO POETS IN PLATO'S REPUBLIC

I left behind the shadow on the cave wall
When I drank the hemlock of Logic's fall
As I tilted that poison bottle
I thought of "Poetics" by Aristotle
My Ethos told me not to harm a soul
My Pathos cried in pain for my heart's whole
So I lodged in Logos like a legal win
Thanatos and Eros my eternal sin...

><

RE: 'TURN ME ON – NOT AROUND' – DAEVID ALLEN

Welcome to the grooming gangs
With wicked smiles and rapist fangs
They are part of our teenage daughters
We offer up for migrant slaughter
When you tell me I can't feel
I'll offer up a brave new deal
I'll keep my hands off your homeland
You can help your own stand
On feet of freedom and liberty
You keep yours and I'll take care of me
Locked inside my warm yurt
No hurt for my just dessert...

RE: MORE

So much depends upon
Your stir tide within
Your embrace of sin
Your attitude
Toward solitude
And rectitude
Ignore the outer winds
Wind toward an inner sun...

RE: LUCKY!

I meet the morning with a poem
Sent by distant friends I'm knowing
Only through their words and mind
But what I find is true and kind.

Walk to the kitchen, pour my cereal
Still stuck here in the Material
Trapped in the daily physical bind
But what I find is true and kind

I want to crawl back in the bed
Surrender to existential dread
Escape the hubbub of life's grind
But what I find is true and kind

So I meet the morning with a poem
What I find is true and kind.....

RE: SO I PUT ON MY COMPASSION FATIGUES

Elder apartheid
The American way
Shunt aside and hide
Those who've seen better days
We shun the unproductive
Refuse to acknowledge death
While wasting our lives
Fearing our last breath

RE: JACK GILBERT'S "BETROTHED"

We are born from a mother's womb
Unalone by definition, we fall into life
Surrounded by a doctor, nurse or midwife.
If we're lucky, we nurture connections
To the cosmos flow though our companions
Be they momentary or lifelong
Singing existence's holy song
Until the last silence is the tomb.

RE: UNSOLICITED E-MAIL

Blocked like a blitzing linebacker
Spam hits my in box then splatters
Against my Maginot Line firewall
Though I don't mind if a few topless selfies
From sites such as Instabang
Slip through to my morning eyes...

RE: I DO NOT KNOW

Butterfly effect flows
From a filthy Seguin Jack in the Box
Through my bloody stools
To a battery of high tech medical tests
To finally finding an answer
Thin as the lining of the small intestine
Raped by bacterial infection,
And now, to heal, to write, to live again
To contribute to the ongoing word storm
Happening in the Jupiter atmosphere
Of your daily appreciated poetic posts...

RE: TRIED GOING OUT WITH ART

She was in love with the Fauves
But infatuated with the Impressionists
She lived a Still Life
Like an Abstract Expressionist.
But ultimate she fell
Under Pop Art's spell
Painted Comic panels green
And moved to Lichtenstein

RE: THE HITCHENS PRINCIPLE

Jesus said to turn the other cheek
But to religious fascists that looks weak
They'll just slash the throat
On their God's command then gloat
All religions sail in the same boat
Some leak more than others but all float

RE: HOW I LOST MY FAITH (IN PREACHERS)
– A NEIL A DAY FREE VERSE

I never had faith in Preachers
Unless they worshipped Mother Earth
More than nuns, teachers,
Or even women who give birth.
Faith is a faster tractor to defeat death
Off which the wise ones look before they lept...

RE: WE CARRY FLOWERS,SONGS,

I can only measure what is gone
By the space inside my soul
What is the size of emptiness
When your whole world is a hole?

I can only find joy in moments
Where I forget my past mistakes
What is the weight of happiness
When your whole world feels fake?

I can only scare the ghosts away
When I invite them in my spirit
To watch the play within a play
To know death is to fear it.

I carry so many unheard songs
Unread poems, unblossomed flowers
I sometime think I've lived too long
I dread the tick tock drip of hours

The taste of life is sweet and sours
Tart to my heart's waning powers

RE: THINK AGAIN

Deification of dead poets may indeed suck
But when life is drained from the living
Through devices become vices
Better not to duck
Time to keep giving.
Some radicals join ISIS
Some join an alleged rebellion
Really a co-opted corporate war Janus.
You may hate the raving orange hellion
Steering our dying empire like Nero
But his lies are the ugly honest face
Of a sick violent materialistic society
That subconsciously finally
Decided rather than pretend to be the world's hero
It would show its bloody fangs for posterity.
As to the role of writing
In an era of endless back biting
When people wonder if it's worth fighting
I say read Orwell
He had the keys to this hell
Not 1984 but Down and Out in Paris and London
A book which made me glad I never worked in a kitchen
And read Auden's tribute to Yeats
To learn about the poetic greats
Then quote Shakespeare's Julius Caesar
"Yon Cassius hath a lean and hungry look"
Wonder why you should write another book
Or when a fat wheelchair bound homeless
Begs you for money at Wal-Mart
And your revulsion starts
Remember this life is priceless
And what you do with it is your choice

RE: EXPECTATIONS /DISAPPOINTMENTS

Perhaps it is better to have never dreamed big things
When crushed by the reality the highway of life brings...

>︵︿︵<

RE: EARTH BENEATH ME WHILE I AM ABOVE

It's never too late to love
After loss has its say and place
Solitude and grief may haunt your face
But living for now is a gift from above
Embrace today with wisdom and grace..

RE: 'THE HIGHWAYMEN' REVIEW: GRUMPY OLD MEN ON THE TRAIL OF GLAMOROUS KILLERS – THE NEW YORK TIMES

High Noon was about the Communist witch hunt
Gary Cooper as a weak lawman
John Wayne hated it, called Coop a c—t
Remade his own versions
Where he killed the Mexicans and Indians
And history proves, by the way,
Like J Edgar Hoover Clyde Barrow was gay
So what is the meaning of it all?
Hollywood glamour is a lie and a fraud

RE: SHOES

Never wear cowboy boots in London
Unless you want sore feet
Also when you see homeless on a city street
Look at the shoes they wear on the median
If they're nicer than your pair
Don't give them money—just compare

RE: ONCE THIS WAS FRONTIER WORLD

Coping with the loss of Utopia
Time to lose our myopia
Society was always dystopia
There were no Good Old Days
The past is a cataract haze
We hope the future will amaze
But doubt and fear are ablaze
Mass shooters quote from the pyre
"I am the god of hellfire"
As our hippie hopes expire....

RE: 49 REASONS TO LOVE

Fifteen hugs a day
Keep evil at bay
As we kneel to pray
Drive demons away
May love descend and stay...

RE: EMOTIONAL WAVES

Earth isn't the same Earth of our ancestors
Our technology fills it daily
With radio waves, microwaves,
Waves the government denies exists.
All disrupt our bodies which are mostly fluid
A sack of blood and bones
Not built to withstand the silent stones
Thrown at us every second.
My emotions range from anger to blank distance
But instead I try to hide from existence...

RE: STORIES IN OUR STARS

In a museum in Peru
My now dead friend Nelson
Laughed at the native constellations
I said "Dude, of course to us they're new
They had their own nation
In the Southern Hemisphere
They saw things differently here"
He looked startled and replied
"That thought just blew my mind"....

Dedicated to Nelson Jesus Barquet

RE: "THE SPIRITUAL DISCIPLINE OF SOLITUDE"

God is the universe
Knowing no gender
To the power of the Oneness
I surrender

RE: NO SPACE IS TOO SMALL FOR PERMACULTURE

When your plant is edible
And you eat it like an animal
Does it scream?
Do you kill its green dream?

RE: IN OUR HOUSE, OUR CAT RULES

She IS a psychic simple tyrant
Who dissolves human cant
As she cleans herself obsessively
While I wean myself aggressively
From the lies I write as I lie here
Refusing to stir for fear
My lover might awaken
As in her dreams she's shaken
By unknown spirit twitches
The soft feline bewitches
She has to control her pose
Until her cat butt rests in my nose
And I realize all my human wiles
Dissolve in her Cheshire smiles....

RE: A ROOM OF ONE'S OWN (2019)

Respect to all women
Who nurture by nature
Without whom we men
Born to rage and ravage
Would revert to the savage
Insecure, impure, immature
May your holy female energy
Bring us sacred synergy...

RE: IT IS GOOD TO GET LOST

Morning freeze
Follows evening ease
Love's squeeze
Awakes to bitter breeze

Last night's dreams
Haunted past seams
Untold reams
Of pages unseen

Icy windshield
To warm water yields
A teary slush
March mush

When April arrives
If our bodies survive
Poetry will thrive
In our protected hive

Until then stay warm
Avoid past harm
And future pain
Certain as April rain....

RE: SUNSHINE SUPERPOWERS!

They say "Go to the light"
When people seek Spirit
It's an eternal fight
Best not to fear it
So when you hear it
Blind and deafen
Know you are merely human...

Re: An emotional intelligence primer in the form of a tender illustrated poem about our capacity for love, Marcus Aurelius's key to living fully, and more

RETITLED: EMOTIONAL INTELLIGENCE

My heart is a public toilet
My heart is a steaming stream
My heart is a full urinal
Where Duchamp took a dump
A fountain of regrets. A mountain
Crowded as Everest at peak times
Where morons queue to die.
My urethra is connected to all
Sharing a Yellow River
Pumping intermittently.
My heart winds through China
My head an aqueduct in Ancient Rome
Below me an ancient gypsy
Cures my impotence
Like a character in Satyricon
Heart dead and gone...

(With apologies to any delicate sensiblities)

RE: "BEFORE QUIET" BY HAZEL HALL

NO QUIET

I have a new kitten
He attacks my feet
Perhaps I should wear mittens
Or toss him in the street.

He scratches up my leg
Tears my girlfriend's arm
We need to calm him down a peg
Before I do him harm

But suddenly he calms
Jumps on my lap and purrs
I hold him in my palms
My love for him stirs

I know he only needs to play
So I decide to let him stay
He makes me feel again
Even if it's just pretend...

RE: THE FIRST FALL(WAS THE GREATEST IN CAMUS' THE FALL

The judge penitent
Who was a successful defense attorney
Addresses the reader directly
About where he's been sent
When he fails after all.

I preferred The Stranger
But still felt in danger
When the Myth of Sisyphus
Rolled me like a boulder that missed.

In my first punk band
I wrote a song called "Big Ambitions"
With the line "Killing an Arab
Is very existential"
My words were a dark scab
Hiding the true emotional.

Now I wonder as I quickly age
What was the point of all those words
I put on page and performed on stage
They haunt me like scrying birds...

RE: AUSTIN WRITERS ROULETTE IS STILL ACCEPTING SUBMISSIONS FOR THE 6/9 "VOLCANIC SUMMER" EVENT

Under normal conditions, summer in Texas is hot
But floods, fires, and tornados are not.
While some say never
Is a long way away
It appears forever
Is veering closer every day.
Facing extinction we brag
Like the Unknown Comic
Our head in a paper bag
A wise cracking cynic
Totally lacking wisdom
About what's to come.
Our oceans are boiling
Our species are broiling
The future for us
May soon look like Venus.
Should we throw ourselves like Pele
Into this volcanic melee?
We are the human sacrifice
We are snake eyes on Earth's dice
The only consolation
Is knowing the situation
Had to happen because
We are who we are
And it was what it was....

RE: LOVE THE JAZZ JAM

Love each other
As sisters and brothers
Love ourselves
As spiritual elves
Love the daily jam
Love what I am
Love you from afar
Love who you are
Love the brook of life
Even love the strife
Love the ocean of hope
Love some good dope
Love the search for paradise
Even if it's Golden lies
Awake with renewed eyes
Dry the fears you cry...

RE: I LIKE DARK HUMOR

A shotgun suicide to the jaw that fails
A bank robber sent to prison for tax evasion
A talking bird who can only say "I can't speak"
Fish in the ocean who say " humans pee in this water"
A surrealist artist tasked with a formal portrait
A silent movie comic with an operatic voice
An Egyptian who mummified his cat for afterlife affection
A man with dementia carrying the nuclear launch codes
The fact Richard Nixon was a Quaker
And Shaker furniture is rustic yet outrageously expensive
When your lover IS the cosmic joker
Pointing out the truth you are not the cream of the crop
You bellow a belly laugh that may never stop
In a meaningless universe where we constantly seek
meaning..

RE: ON THE LIPS OF MARCH

Americans make war on anything
As long as there's money in it–
Weeds, the weather, drugs, terror,
They tell us it's the price of Empire
But deny we are an empire.
Don't cross us
or we'll bomb your garden for breakfast.
Enjoy a drone with your scone.
As for tea, we prefer sweet and instant
As we can't wait to contemplate
Our next business transaction
But for all our prosperity
We can't get no satisfaction...

RE: REBIRTHING

February wildflowers come early to dance
On Texas highways this year
Yet March in its leonine entrance
May soak them in cold rain's fear...

RE: THE WEATHER

I noticed the bluebonnets
Early this year
Beyond any sonnets
It's a sign to fear..

RE: "MUSIC CAN MOVE PEOPLE TO DO THINGS" (JOAN BAEZ)

At the soundboard once at a folk festival
Backstage with a friend.
He said, "She still sounds like she did in the 60s!"
The sound man let out a rueful laugh
"This is what she really sounds like"
And in our ears a horrible caterwauling came.
He quickly punched the Autotune button back on.
"Maybe some dreams are better left back in the 60's"

RE: DANCING TO THE D.J

Just after Peyote
I traversed the universe
With cosmic spirits
Native shamans.
In harsh industrial dance clubs
Corporate wolves
Danced mechanically on cocaine
Bought with profits
Earned by raping
Mother Earth
Strangling her life by the throat.
As they gloat
Prophets hear distant drums
Beat prayers of change
Hopefully not too late....

RE: BREATH, PRAYER AND HEALING

May the air we share
Bring spiritual repair
Bind the wounds that tear
Apart our hearts in tears
To erase our fears...

RE: PEACE IS A VERB

If inner peace and outer peace could neatly align
We'd have no prison walls within our minds
If everyone knew the answer to why we war
Perhaps we could purchase the salve at the store
In a society of universal commodification
An atomized people might be a nation
Instead we pour hatred screeds into screens
Wondering if social media turns us mean
Or perhaps as Hobbes knew all along
Life is nasty, brutish, and not very long.....

>ᢒᡐᡒᡆᡆᢗᡣᢗᢤ

RE: HEARING LOSS

My girlfriend said something to me
But I replied "Huh?"
When I was younger I pretended
Not to hear to wiggle free
But now it's a reality
My hearing is upended
But I can still answer "Duh!"
So she thinks she's got me
To admit she was right.
Presto! We never fight....

RE: FUTURE FICTION FACT

A found poem in a computer file
Makes my hard drive smile
Will it linger a while
Or move to the discard pile...

>☞~☜

RE: I AM WAITING FOR PEACE ON THIS PLANET

The toilet of my heart
Needs a plumber soon
Or I'll spend my life
In a clogged bathroom
Where written on my tomb
The words will start
"He sat alone in strife
With a leaky pipe over two half moons....

>☞~☜

RE: WHAT POETS ARE FOR

Poets bring insights to a society
Always focused on utility..

RE: ADRENOCHROME/IMMORTALISM

It's all in the blood sided eyes
But when Hunter S had enough of the lies
The shotgun clicked– and he died...

><TH>~<TH><

RE: WE NEVER ASKED

Ask someone today
If they're okay
The answer might surprise
But remember to act wise
The question is the point anyway....

><TH>~<TH><

RE: EMOTIONAL JUKEBOX

Joy and sorrow
On life's balance beam
As an acrobat tomorrow
Toward one we may lean
But this day we borrow
Is a chance to dream
So dismount and know
On must go the show....

RE: THE BIG WHITE LIE

Celibacy is unnatural
Hiding behind ritual
These holy men are still mammals
Who act like caged animals
Even beasts in the jungle
Know not to shit their nests
So I don't believe Father knows best....

>rr~rx

RE: I WAS A TEENAGE ADULT

Fast flow of river in the canyons
At the top of the pint (mound in the bottom of the ground
With my songs of glued triumph(when the wings soared...
I was wearing tire tread sandals (small, tight as an acrobat
Heavily tripping on Ecstasy and THC sold separately/ ear
lost
At the exit of this earth where (delightedly at height
Where cheese wheeled ideas roll, roll, rolled
Though happy myths and dark concretes, transfixed by
scrolling breaking news
Take a Croissant Jelly Methodist, dropping five burnt
ostriches
Six soaring aircraft carriers. Seven chemical compounds.
Eight oysters Rockefeller,
Nine named Indians on metal teepees. You should never
give parables
With a pour of Mrs Dash and a ginger beard. Now to lock
the loudness, destroy old lines
Dostoyevsky for Experts....

RE: JANE GOODALL'S LOVELY LETTER TO CHILDREN ABOUT HOW READING SHAPED HER LIFE, PHILOSOPHER MAURICE BLANCHOT ON WRITING AND WHAT IT REALLY MEANS TO SEE

Watch Primates Act
Know for a fact
All humanity
Are merely monkeys...

＞﹏＜

RE: DAVID WHYTE ON LOVE, HERMANN HESSE ON SOLITUDE, THE VALUE OF HARDSHIP, AND HOW TO FIND YOUR DESTINY, NICK CAVE ON ART IN THE AGE OF AI

Has solitude
Turned me rude?
Was Nietzsche a Nazi?
Was Hesse a Buddhist?
As I grow older
Tired and less bolder
Life– the oldest riddle
I'm toast hot off the griddle
With these words I fiddle
Knowledge's holy spittle
China's latest broadcast
From the Dark Side of the Moon
Reminds me future and past
Are only present's anteroom
While I only care to stare
My youth's truth now an empty dare
At the ball toss at the County Fair
I try to win the Teddy Bear
But lose the reason why I care
A loving pair in silent despair....

45

RE: ADDICTED TO SBS

Massacres and petrol sniffing
A planet nearly done
An ozone layer destroyed
Hiding from the sun
Underpaid and underemployed
Lost in apocalyptic riffing
Nowhere to run...

RE: ALL OF THE ABOVE

Give me warm rain from the sky
Maui, Miami, L.A.– but why?
I am a cold blooded creature
Who needs solar radiation as a feature
To keep my blood running fine
I'm a beach Prince in eternal sunshine...

RE: THE CHILDREN KNOW

I know the children who suffer
Because I was one
I prayed for some buffer
From pain and to run.
I learned how to read
Then how to write
But never to bleed
Never to fight.
When the harsh sun
Beat down on my skin
I learned it meant fun
Sweating to win.
My limbs hidden in earth
So hurt and alone
A stranger at birth
Beaten to the bone....

RE: ORIGINAL INFLUENCES

What we really need
Is a Ministry of Brains
Facebook Millennials
Shipped on trains
To sterilization centers
Clipped without pain
So we don't repeat
The same mistakes again...

RE: CAT PURRS

Cats are never bores
But they are attention whores
They accept heavy petting
Without any vetting
The price you always pay:
When they're done they strut away...

RE: BACK MATTER: CHARLES DICKENS GIVES AMERICA A TWO-STAR REVIEW

Yet the sacred cow in mooing choir
Sees the open field as abattoir...

RE: THE FAMILY RE-UNION

Philadelphia was the most populous city
In North America in 1776.
Aleready class distinctions emerged
Among both aristocratic families there
And in Boston and in agricultural
States such as Virginia, yielding a group
Of men known as "The Founding Fathers"
None of whom worshipped Goddess based
Religions nor exhibited equality toward anyone
Not a white property owning male.
The currency they created
Was based on the decimal system
To facilitate ease of use in commerce.
While royalty was indeed banned,
The class system existed and is considered
The root cause of the Civil War
As Industrial Northern economic interests
Sought to dominate then eliminate
The paramount Social ill of slavery
Upon which the agrarian South
With its plantation mentality
Degraded individuals daily.
So I question definitions
Based in flawed readings of history
As to the Torah– Google
"Slave trading families
In Wilmington, Delaware"

RE: DROUGHT&WALLS

Sargon of Akkad
Banned by Patreon
Free speech Pile on

Torrential rain and floods
Stops flow of endless goods
Boil water orders in Austin

Lost in all utopias
Human greed ropes ya
Cynical sin wins...

RE: DROPPING BIBLES INSTEAD OF BOMBS

I hated High School but loved philosophy
Drawn to the darker existentialists
I believed Sartre when he said
"Hell is other people"
Like Camus's Sisyphus
I fancied myself uniquely rolling
The burdensome boulder of life up every hill
Only to realize later that my hell was myself
Heaven was where I could free my mind
Beyond good and evil. While the devil?
He lived in the man who shot John Lennon.
I stood on a mossy hill that December
Holding hands in a circle with a high school friend
Who three years later would become my college lover
Teaching me that heaven is truly loving another
And hell is losing that feeling.
Now my current woman lies snoozing beside me
And I pray for all souls to sleep peacefully,
Live joyfully, and never suffer want.
But then I wake up.

RE: DANCING WITH DEPRESSION&DESPAIR

Punk rock nihilism
Is soured romanticism.
Austin was an epicenter of youth crying
But now the old school is dying
Of old age. Depression, drugs,
Suicide, lack of hugs,
Early cynicism swept under rugs.
Optimism curdles to DT bugs.
Anger may be an energy
But the second law of thermodynamics
Ensures final entropy
Will win and make you sick....

RE: HOMELESS R US

I feel more in tune with the homeless
Than the indifferent prosperous
Or the selfish mass populous.
I've walked among them in our cities
Their tent encampments hardly pretty
Yet they retain a dignity–
A freedom of action and soul
Missing in the heartless hole
Within the conforming whole.
So between the elite and the street
Is where I live to greet
Everyday and everyone I meet

RE: WE WANT TO KNOW WHEN WE CAME FROM

Bertrand Russell said "If God created the universe, who created God?"
Albert Einstein said, "God does not play dice with the universe"
Stephen Hawking said "The universe is shaped like a shuttlecock"
Does he mean God plays badminton with the universe?
Or the universe is a bad backyard children's game?
Maybe Earth is a tether ball and the Sun its stable central pole.
Then Hawking asks "What is South of the South Pole."
Now the answer's easy– empty space.
Of course, he had the academic chair once held by Issac Newton
While I'm just lying on my couch.
But from this seat, quantum theories about the origin of the universe
Or multiverse or even this free verse
Bump up against our too human limitations.
Scientists keep devising ever more elaborate explanations
For what may simply lie beyond our comprehension.
I came from my mother's womb
I'll one day lose my heat energy and entropy into a tomb
Until then, people can launch all the Hubble telescopes,
Build Large Hadron Colliders, deep space probes,
Formulate mathematical equations, wear Sage robes
Pontificating on the unknowable origin of everything
While I wonder if whatever forces rule this realm
Rolled seven or snake eyes when they seized the helm.

RE: SEPTEMBER 1, 1939 BY W. H. AUDEN

Black Mirror starring Miley Cyrus. Watch it on your I-Pad
thru Hulu. Take licensed cabs for security. We live in
a prison reality show, loving our chains. Technology
promised to bring us together but binds us in Virtual
Solitary Confinement. Hell May be other people but I'd
rather suffer in the Seventh Circle with flesh than faux
Facebook likes or YouTube banning free speech for fear
of offending the incoming consumer. Like Neo shaking in
the dentist chair, we affect the droll doll attitude of Keanu
Reeves who said it best that at death those who loved you
will mourn-maybe. Quantum realities leap from unknown
valences every nanosecond where Choice really isn't
voluntary or even known. Meanwhile the unknown awaits
you every second of this existence. Slam down your phony
IPhone world on the hard pavement of the present as
Mother Earth screams "the sky is falling, I am dying" while
billions of haughty hominids await their fate like factory
farmed chickens. Which came first- the egg or the square
peg? D-Day was yesterday, the war starts tomorrow, today
I pray to escape this vocabulary trap.

RE: LETTING THINGS GO, A POEM BY O.L. BUZZERD

I can't be bothered
To shower or shave
What's the point
This near the grave
I may not even
Leave the house today
I've got enough food
Why not just stay
It's a hundred degrees
On my front porch
Like sticking your head
In The Olympic torch
I'll win a gold medal
In lazy sloth
Sit here sipping
Some hazy broth
My lifelong goals
Already gone
Best to rest
Embrace my yawn
Drop this iPad
Kitten on my chest
Say good day
It's time to rest....

RE: IT IS NOT THE COUNTING OF THE DAYS

What can be said in New Year rhymes
We look back on last year's times

Some good, some bad, yet still we strive
Mostly glad to be alive

For next year's hopes and dreams we pine
As we sing Auld Lang Syne

Remember those whose souls did pass
Shed a tear then raise a glass

Look forward to a better year
Dance away from pain and fear

Awake to a year new in name
But realize life's still the same....

ABOUT THE AUTHOR

PoetKen Jones has written, published, and performed his original poetry and music for over forty years in venues around the world. This book is his 8th full length published poetry collection. He earned a Master of Arts in English/Creative Writing from the University of Texas at Austin at the age of 23 and has been a Finalist for the West Chester Poet's Prize, Winner of the Houston Fringe Festival Critic's Choice Award and a two time Pushcart Prize nominee, among other achievements. He is also a licensed attorney in the state of Texas and an honors graduate of the University of Southern California Gould School of Law, who currently works as a country lawyer in South and Central Texas.

See www.poetken.com

Photo by Douglas Alan Wills, Esquire

PoetKen disobeying the rules as usual, March 29, 2018 in Jerome, Arizona

www.ingramcontent.com/pod-product-compliance
Lightning Source LLC
Chambersburg PA
CBHW032057040426
42449CB00007B/1115